David and Goliath

I Samuel 17:1-51

Retold by Pamela Broughton
Illustrated by Tom LaPadula

A GOLDEN BOOK® • NEW YORK

There was a war in the land of Israel. The Philistine armies had come to fight, and they were ready and waiting in their mountaintop camp.

King Saul and the men of Israel were ready, too.
They waited atop another mountain, across the valley.

A champion came out of the Philistine camp. He was a giant named Goliath of Gath. He cried to the men of Israel, "Choose a champion for yourselves. If he is able to kill me, then the Philistines will be your servants. But if I kill him, then you shall be our servants. Give me a man to fight!"

When Saul and the men of Israel heard these words, they were greatly afraid. They did not have a man who could defeat the giant.

Now there was a boy named David, and he was the youngest of eight sons. While three of his older brothers served in the army, David took care of his father's sheep in Bethlehem.

One day David's father sent for him. He told David to take some food to his brothers and their captain, and to bring back news of the war.

David awoke early the next morning. He took the food and set out for King Saul's camp.

When he arrived, David left the food with the
supply keeper. Then he went to find his brothers.

As David talked with his brothers, Goliath came out again to challenge the army of Israel.

When the men of Israel saw Goliath, they were frightened and ran away.

Some men said to David, "Do you see this giant? King Saul will give riches and his own daughter in marriage to the man who can kill him."

And David said, "Who is this Philistine to threaten
the army of the living God?"

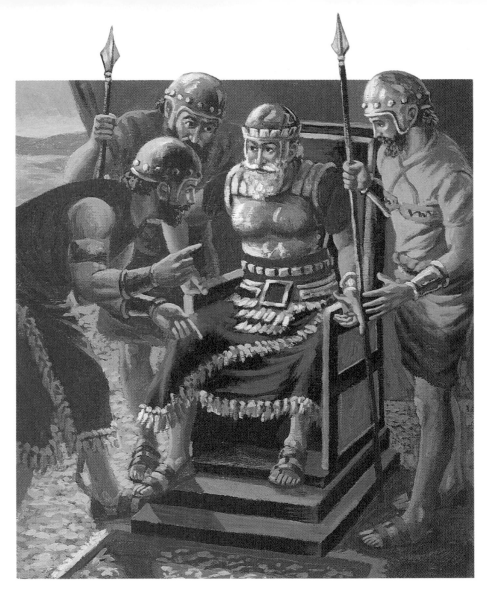

When the people heard David's words, they ran to tell them to King Saul. Then Saul sent for David.

David said, "Let no one fear Goliath. I will go and fight this man."

But Saul said, "You cannot fight him. You are just a boy, and he is a trained soldier."

David said to King Saul, "I kept my father's sheep. A lion came, and it took a lamb out of the flock. And I went out after the lamb and took it from the lion's mouth. I killed the lion. This giant shall be like that lion. The Lord who delivered me from the lion will deliver me from this Philistine."

And Saul said to David, "Go, and the Lord be with you."

King Saul gave David his own armor to wear in the battle. David tried it on. Then he said, "I cannot wear this armor. I am not used to it."

And he took off Saul's armor.

David took up his staff. He picked five smooth stones out of a brook and put them in his shepherd's bag. He took his sling and went out to meet Goliath.

When the Philistine saw David with his staff, he
said, "Am I a dog that you come to me with sticks?"

David answered, "You come to me with a sword and a shield. But I come to you in the name of the Lord, the God of the army of Israel. This day the Lord will deliver you into my hand, that all the earth may know there is a God in Israel."

David put his hand in his bag and took out a stone. He put the stone in his sling and took careful aim. Then he swung the sling and let go. The stone struck the Philistine's forehead, and Goliath fell to the ground.

David ran and took Goliath's sword and cut off the giant's head.

When the Philistines saw that their champion was dead, they grew afraid and ran away. The men of Israel ran after them and drove them off.

So David defeated the Philistines with a sling and a stone, and the help of the living God.